INFO BANK

ANIMALS

First published by Miles Kelly Publishing Ltd
Bardfield Centre, Great Bardfield
Essex, CM7 4SL

2 4 6 8 10 9 7 5 3 1

Editor
Isla MacCuish

Designer
Venita Kidwai

Editorial Director
Paula Borton

Art Director
Clare Sleven

Picture Research
Liberty Newton

British Library Cataloguing-in-Publication Data
A catalogue record for this book is available from the British Library

ISBN 1-84236-153-8
Printed in Hong Kong

www.mileskelly.net
info@mileskelly.net

Acknowledgements

The publishers would like to thank the following artists whose work appears in this book:

Scenes:
Mike Saunders, Luigi Galante Studios.

Small illustrations:
Jim Channell (Bernard Thornton Artists), Alan Harris,
Sarah Smith (Linden Artists), Rudi Vizi, Paul Williams.

All photographs from Miles Kelly archives.

INFO BANK

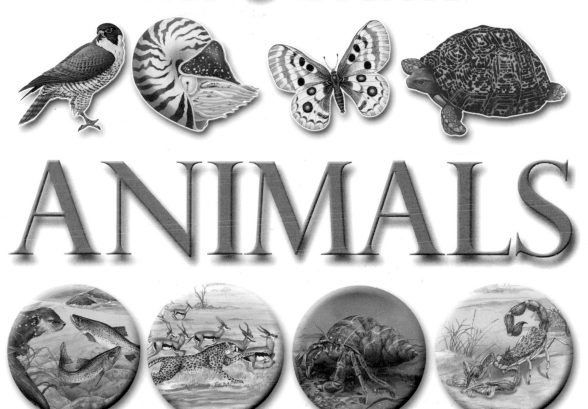

ANIMALS

STEVE PARKER

Miles Kelly
PUBLISHING

CONTENTS

ANIMAL HABITATS

Sea and Ocean
Far out at sea, there is nowhere to hide. The water stretches almost endlessly in every direction, and so danger can approach from every direction, too. However animals of the open ocean still manage to carry out the essentials of life, finding their way, catching food and even building their own shelters.

Shore
Where land meets sea is the world's most changeable habitat. Tides rise and fall, rain turns salty water fresh, then disappears in drying winds and hot sun, until storm waves smash the shore to pieces. Sea creatures must be tough and nimble, or protected in shells, ready to eat anything the sea throws up for them.

River & Lake
Water is vital for plant life, and where plants grow, animals are there to eat them. This happens along the banks of rivers and lakes, which also provide shelter for nests and families. The water currents bring food too, for aquatic creatures. The river's links with the sea mean swimming migrations in various directions.

Swamp

The in-between world of marshes, swamps and other wetlands suits both land and water creatures. Many spend their early lives in the water, then come out on to land as adults, or even take to the air. Migrants fly in to take advantage of plentiful food in summer. They leave as the plants wither and pools freeze in winter.

Rainforest

No habitat is richer in wildlife than the tropical rainforest. Animals are active day and night, all through the year, as they find food, set up nests and other homes, or try to attract breeding partners. However, predators and other dangers lurk behind almost every leaf.

Woodland

Spring in the wood is a busy time. As the shoots and leaves appear, creatures shake off the winter, feed, and begin to raise their young. Birds and butterflies flit among the branches by day, while bats and owls take over at night. The old leaves on the woodland floor hide a miniature but fierce struggle for survival.

Grassland

With few trees or rocks to use for shelter, animals of the grasslands have two main ways of survival. Some are big and fast, to catch prey or escape predators. Others dig and burrow to make homes and shelters. Many grasslands suffer from droughts and wildfires.

Desert

Even the world's driest places are home to plant and animal life. Creatures have many special features to cope with thorny plant food, the lack of water, scorching sun, shifting sands, and hunters. Many of the smaller predators are poisonous, since prey is very scarce, and they must make sure of catching it.

Tundra

The tundra is the cold, windy, treeless land in the far north of the world, bordered by polar seas. The short summer sees light and warmth, when animals migrate from the south to feed on the plant growth. But they soon return as the winter sets in. Creatures who stay must endure months of freezing temperatures.

Mountain

Moving around on mountains is difficult. Birds can soar above the crags, but land animals must be sure-footed on the steep, slippery slopes. Also, mountain weather can change in minutes, from warm, calm and sunny, to a howling gale and snowy blizzard.

HOW TO USE THE SUBJECT LINKS

Navigate your way through this book using the colour-coded lozenges located in the bottom right hand corner of every spread. Flip through the pages, matching colours and sub-headings, and you can compare and contrast themes such as migration, growing up and communication across ten different animal habitats.

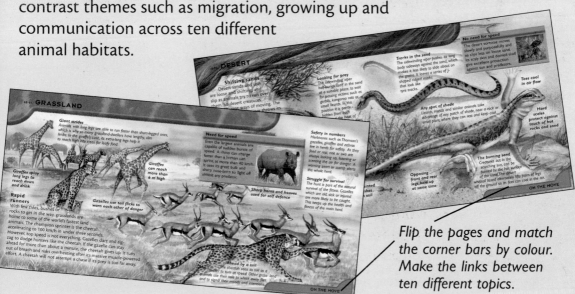

Flip the pages and match the corner bars by colour. Make the links between ten different topics.

SEA AND OCEAN

Large front flippers for swimming

Flattened underside of shell (plastron)

Smaller rear flippers act as rudders

Domed upper side of shell (carapace)

Flippers and flukes
Dolphins live high-speed lives, swimming and leaping with great rapidity. They also sometimes move in mixed shoals with several other kinds, or species, of dolphins. The dolphin swims by swishing its tail flukes up and down. The front flippers, which are its 'arms', are mainly for steering at slow speed and are usually folded against the body when going fast.

Safe in their shells
The turtle's strong shell is made of a bony inner layer covered by plates of tough horn on the outside. The skin is leathery and covered in hard scales. Courting turtles do a slow, ponderous 'dance' in the sea as they court and mate. Then the female swims hundreds of kilometres back to a beach, where she digs a hole in the sand to lay her eggs.

Tail flukes have pointed tips so water slips past them easily

Courtship in the water

Ocean creatures attract a mate at breeding time, just like animals on land. Sounds and scents travel much farther in the water than in air, and sounds go faster too, so many ocean-dwellers make use of these to draw the attention of a breeding partner. Whales, dolphins and porpoises, in particular, make a whole range of squeaks, clicks and grunts as they court. As they come closer to each other they use touch as well, stroking and caressing their partners.

Suitable sounds

The dolphin's courtship calls are different from the many other sounds it makes, which are used for finding food by echolocation, or for contacting other members of its shoal.

Courtship colours

Cuttlefish normally live alone but come together in small shoals to breed. Each uses colour and pattern to signal its readiness to mate as waves of black, yellow and brown pass rapidly along its body.

Giant shoal

Fish such as herring have no obvious protection except for their darting speed — and being in a huge group. The colony moves together, twisting and turning almost as one. The effect is to make the shoal resemble a single massive animal, a 'super-organism' that could confuse or frighten off predators.

Seen from above

Shoaling fish are more likely to be seen than lone fish by predators flying above the water's surface, such as gannets.

When the gannet comes near to the shoal, the flashes and glints from the herrings' shiny scales make it difficult to pick out one victim

Nowhere to hide

The open ocean is a very exposed place. There are no rocks or seaweeds for shelter or hiding. Many animals use camouflage or swimming skills to avoid being eaten. But some, like sea turtles and the nautilus, have protective shells. The nautilus is a type of animal called a mollusc, a cousin of the octopus and of the various shellfish on the shore such as mussels, clams and whelks. It builds its shell out of calcium and other minerals it takes from the sea water. The nautilus spends its day resting before going out to hunt at night, grabbing on to its next meal with waving tentacles.

Jet propulsion

The nautilus swims by sucking water slowly into a chamber inside its body. Then it squirts the water out rapidly through a narrow exit. As the water jet squirts one way, the nautilus is pushed the other way. The nautilus also uses bubbles of gas to help it rise and sink.

Hunting in the dark

The nautilus is active at night. It hunts squid, fish and other prey using its huge eyes and sense of touch. It detects ripples made by moving animals and grabs victims with its numerous tentacles, passing meals to its mouth in the centre of the tentacle ring.

Fleshy cloak-like mantle covers much of body

Tentacles grab prey

Huge eyes for hunting by night

Animal's body is in last section of shell

Squid are molluscs like the nautilus but have shells inside the body

SEA AND OCEAN

Danger all around

Land animals face the threat of predators approaching mainly from the sides, or perhaps from above, in the form of an eagle or hawk. But in the sea, danger can appear from any direction – including from the dark depths below. One of the ocean's most fearsome hunters is the shark. It detects the blood or body fluids of an injured animal from many kilometres away, and quickly moves in for the kill.

Shark's pectoral (side) fin is used for rising or descending

Fish such as the shark swish the tail from side to side to swim

The slowest hunter

Jellyfish can swim only slowly, as they squeeze or pulsate the main umbrella-shaped part of the body, the bell. But their long trailing tentacles catch and sting many small creatures such as fish and prawns.

Front flippers used for steering

Closing in

At first the shark relies on scent to find its victim. As it closes in, its sight becomes more important, and it also detects ripples of electricity in the water, given off by the muscles of its victim.

Whale's hairless skin slips easily through water

Parasite pests

Like land mammals, sea mammals such as whales suffer from blood-sucking parasites like whale lice. Other parasites, like barnacles, simply attach to and live on the whale, using it as a base but not sucking its blood.

No light to see by

On the bottom of the deep sea, there is almost no light at all. Some creatures here have huge eyes to peer in the gloom. Others find food mainly by smell and touch, and also by sensing weak pulses of electricity given off into the water by the active muscles of their prey.

ON THE HUNT

SEA AND OCEAN

Yearly journey

Most great whales, like the blue, fin, sei, grey and humpback, make yearly migrations. In spring they swim north or south, away from the tropics towards the colder waters near the poles. Here, their food such as fish and shrimp-like krill breed in incredible numbers, due to the rich nutrients stirred up by ocean currents. In autumn the well-fed whales swim back towards the warmer waters of the tropics for winter, where the females give birth to their young, or calves.

Sounding out the surroundings

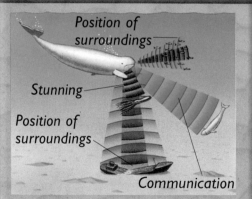

Position of surroundings

Stunning

Position of surroundings

Communication

Small whales, like beluga whales, can use sonar in several different ways. They can can use it to communicate with other whales, or to sense the positions of surrounding objects. Stronger sonar waves are used to stun enemies or prey.

Thick layer of fatty blubber under skin keeps in whale's body heat

Throat grooves

The humpback has grooves or pleats of skin on its throat. This allows the throat to expand like a balloon as the whale gulps in a huge mouthful of water, to filter small food items from it.

Courtship calls

In great whales like the humpback, usually only the male sings at breeding time. He 'hangs' still in the water at a depth of 20-40 m and produces a series of moans, squeals, squeaks and groans that last for up to 20 minutes. Then he sings the whole song again. The sounds travel for dozens of kilometres through the sea.

Calf (young whale) stays close by its mother

Tail flukes are mainly skin and muscle (they lack bones)

Natural noises

Whales may listen to natural underwater sounds, such as currents swirling around rocks, or through narrow channels, to help them navigate on their migration.

ON MIGRATION

Seabird colony

Gannets are among many seabirds that breed in huge groups or colonies. The colony, or gannetry, is a noisy and crowded place. The birds swoop down in their hundreds, attacking and pecking any other animal that comes near. A gannetry may contain as many as 50,000 nests.

Parent gannets take food back to their young in the nest

Webbed feet for swimming

Untidy nests

The gannet's nest is on a ledge or steep slope, on an offshore islet well out of reach of land-based predators. It is also spaced apart from surrounding nests so neighbours are just out of pecking range. The nest is an untidy mound of seaweed and various bits of debris.

Processed food

Shore birds such as the gannet catch and swallow fish and other food, sometimes far out at sea. When they return to the nests, the food is already partly digested and soft. The parent bird regurgitates (brings up) this prepared meal for its nestlings.

Too many to eat

One threat facing a baby animal is the predators who want to eat it. Along coasts and shores there are many hunters. One way of reducing the danger is to breed in a big colony, all at the same time. There are many parents to guard against enemies. There are so many youngsters that they cannot all be eaten. Predators are swamped with too much food and so many offspring must survive.

Nesting alone

Coastal birds of prey such as sea eagles nest in single pairs. The eyrie (nest) is a large pile of twigs and sticks in a tree or on a steep crag. The female sits on the eggs to incubate them, with the male taking over for short periods while she goes off to catch fish.

Puffins breed in crowded colonies, with each pair of birds hatching a single chick

Oystercatcher prises open shellfish with its strong beak

Taking the plunge

Most seas and oceans teem with fish, shellfish, worms and other creatures, which are a plentiful source of food. But there are also dangers such as sharks and poisonous jellyfish. So some animals have dual lives. They rest and breed on land, but hunt for food in the water. They vary from otters and small water shrews to larger seals, sea-lions and crocodiles. The shores of lakes, rivers and seas are ideal places for this type of land-and-water lifestyle.

Wings for swimming

Penguins have strong wings but they cannot fly – at least, not in the air. However, they make flapping movements very similar to flying when underwater. The penguin holds its beak, head and neck out straight in front and folds its feet back, to make itself more streamlined, for greater swimming speed.

Catching oysters

The oystercatcher feeds not only on oysters, but on mussels, clams, limpets and many other kinds of shellfish, also crabs, shrimps and worms. It has a chisel-like bill and strong neck muscles to stab and strike its food, carefully picking its spot to crack or lever open the shell.

Storm petrel swoops to hover just above surface and look for food

Supreme swimmers
Grey seals look clumsy on land, as they wriggle up on to the rocks to rest. But when they dive into the water they swim with amazing speed and grace, swishing the rear end of the body and 'kicking' each rear flipper in turn. The front ones are used for sudden stops and turns.

An oceanic life
Storm petrels only come on to land to breed. They spend the rest of their lives along coasts or far out at sea, feeding and sleeping on the wing or floating on the waves.

Male seal (bull) is twice as heavy as female (cow)

Seal's smooth, streamlined body slips easily through water

Fish hunters
Seals feed mainly on fish and the grey seal, which grows more than 2 m long, needs about 10 kg each day. It takes mainly larger fish such as salmon, cod and whiting.

Making a meal of rubbish

The sea washes up a regular supply of old seaweed, dead fish and other bits and pieces of rotting plants and animals. This is all food for the scavengers of the shore, such as the many kinds of crabs. They sift through the mud, sand, pebbles and debris, and eat anything nutritious, helping to keep the coast clear of nature's leftovers and rubbish.

Hard-cased crab

Shore crabs have shell-like body cases to protect them not only against the beaks, teeth and suckers of predators, but also against coastal hazards such as crashing waves and rolling pebbles. If the crab's leg is trapped under a rock, it can detach itself without too much harm.

Many sets of mouthparts sort and filter food

Simple animals called sea squirts stick to rocks, taking in a continuous flow of water to sieve for plankton

First pair of limbs specialized as strong pincers

Sucked to death

The starfish is a slow but relentless predator. It wraps its arms around the shell of a victim such as a mussel, grips with its hundreds of sucker-tipped tube feet, and begins to pull hard. As some tube feet tire, others resume their grip, in relays. Finally the shellfish gapes open and the starfish turns its own stomach inside out to digest the exposed flesh.

A good grip

Many sea creatures, including starfish, limpets and octopuses, use suckers. The surrounding water makes a good seal and presses hard around the edge of each sucker, so that it is more effective than it would be in air.

Mouth in middle of underside of starfish

Jet propulsion

The scallop's two-part shell is not only for protection. The scallop flaps the two halves or valves together and swims jerkily over the sea bed propelled by jets of water.

Slippery skin
The butterfish is well named from its slippery, slimy skin covered in small, flexible scales. This feature allows it to wriggle through seaweed, between boulders and even across rocks from one pool to another. It eats small worms, shrimps, baby fish and other prey.

Distinctive row of about 12 black spots along each side of upper body

Scales are small, leathery and embedded in skin

Worm's home
The peacock worm makes its house from sand and mud glued with hardened mucus. The tentacles withdraw if danger threatens.

Beautiful plumes
The colourful 'feathers' of the peacock worm are really frilly, antennae-like tentacles around its head. They are coated with sticky mucus that traps tiny floating pieces of food. The mucus slides slowly down into the worm's mouth, carrying its micro-meals with it.

Shells – own and stolen

Shores and coasts are some of the most dangerous habitats. Giant waves crash down with a force of many tonnes, rolling boulders as big as houses or crumbling cliffs into rubble, as storms batter the land. This is why so many shore creatures have strong shells for protection. Many are also fixed in place so that the sea cannot sweep them away and smash them against the rocks.

Antennae detect movements and waterborne scents

Sensing surroundings
Crabs and similar sea creatures have short feelers or antennae on their heads. These sense not only movements and currents in the water, but also blood from an injured or dying fish.

Recycled shell
Unlike other hard-cased crabs, the hermit crab has a soft body. So it climbs inside the old shell of another creature, usually a whelk, and uses this as a second-hand, mobile home.

The riverbank nursery

Many baby animals grow up along rivers and lakes – especially the young of waterbirds like swans and grebes. The young birds or chicks stay in their nest at first, where they are warm and dry, and fed and protected by their parents. As the youngsters become bigger and stronger, they can their leave the nest for short periods. They learn to swim and dive in the river, and to cope with the waves and currents.

Wide bill

The swan's large, wide beak can pick up all kinds of food like grass, leaves, reeds and other water plants, and also water creatures such as snails, insects and worms.

Male guarding the nest

The male swan, known as the cob, stays near to defend the nest and his family against marauding animals. If danger approaches, he spreads his wings, bends his neck, opens his beak, hisses loudly and pecks at enemies.

Safe cygnets

Baby swans are called cygnets. Two or three weeks after they hatch, they start to leave the nest for short trips. At first they ride on their mother's back among her feathers. Gradually they learn to swim and find their own food. The cygnets moult their baby feathers, grow adult feathers, and are ready to fly about eight weeks after hatching.

Salmon leaps out of water to catch flies for food

Female on the nest
The swans' nest is a large mound of reeds, sedges and similar water plants. The mother swan, called the pen, plucks feathers from her own body to make a lining that is soft and warm.

Paired for life
Many birds choose a different breeding partner each year, but the female and the male swan 'pair for life', and they raise about four chicks each year. Some seabirds also pair for life, like the huge albatross (above). Albatrosses breed much more slowly than swans. They only raise one chick every two years.

Sharing babycare
Horned grebes build a large nest of floating water weeds. The female and male take turns to sit on, or incubate, the eggs. Both the parents also feed the chicks and take turns to give them piggyback rides.

Grebe's sharp beak catches small fish, frogs and similar creatures

Nest is anchored by plants growing up from below

Male grebe feeds while female sits on eggs

Together for a while

Among the many different kinds of animal parents, it is the mammals who care for their young most, and for the longest time. The mother feeds her babies on her milk, and in some types of mammals, the father also helps to protect his family. Harbour (common) seals are mammals and sometimes swim from the sea using their flipper-shaped limbs, up rivers into lakes, to raise their young.

On guard

Each female harbour seal gives birth to a single pup. She feeds it on her milk and guards it closely for several weeks. Gradually, the pup learns to catch its own prey and becomes independent by about eight weeks after birth.

Thick layer of blubber (fat) under skin keeps in body heat

Seal mother hauls out (comes on to land) to rest and feed her pup

Learning to swim

The seal pup does not have to learn to swim. It can paddle and flap its flippers strongly almost from birth, by built-in behaviour or instinct.

Salmon leap to avoid being caught by otter

Otter twists and turns after fish, frogs and other prey

Learning to feed

Bear cubs learn from their mother about how to find food and stay safe. They sniff and examine many kinds of foods, from berries and shoots to the honey in wild bees' nests. By trial and error they learn what is good to eat and what is not. Freshly dead salmon in the river provide an unexpected meal, and the cub remembers the time and place so that it can return next year.

Tiny babies

Newborn bear cubs are tiny compared to their huge mother, almost small enough to fit into a coffee mug, and weighing only 0.5 kg compared to her great bulk of 200 kg. They stay in the den at first but start to venture out and explore as a family after a couple of months.

Fish is scooped out with paw or grabbed in mouth

Fish feast

Bears gather at rivers as salmon migrate in from the sea. The fish produce their spawn (eggs) and, exhausted, soon die – providing easy food for the waiting bears.

Food for winter

Brown bears usually sleep deeply in their dens in winter. They live off a thick, fatty, blubber-like layer just under their skin, which helps to keep them warm and provide survival energy during the long cold season.

RIVER AND LAKE

Short-distance journey

River dolphins (below) such as the boutu of the Amazon, make small and regular journeys along the rivers where they live with the seasons. They use their long and flexible fish-like bodies to swim very fast after migrating fish and other sources of food, making clicks of sound and listening to the echoes to locate prey.

Up stream battle

On their migration up river, salmon swish their long, flexible bodies to swim against the current, leaping up rapids and waterfalls.

Sockeye salmon

Eggs in the bed

Most birds and mammals put their energy and resources into producing just a few offspring, and feeding and protecting these. But most fish, like salmon, give no parental care. They put their resources into producing thousands of tiny eggs, and simply leave these to develop on their own. The female salmon releases her eggs, or spawn, and the male fertilizes them with his sperm, or milt. The eggs settle in the gravel of the stream or lake bed and begin their development.

Female North Pacific salmon lays eggs

Long-distance journey

Common eels hatch in the Sargasso Sea in the west Atlantic and drift to Europe with the ocean currents, developing as larvae. They grow up in freshwater rivers and lakes, and swim back to the Sargasso Sea to mate.

4 years

3 years

Sargasso Sea

1 year   2 years

Return to home

Fish such as sockeye salmon grow from tiny eggs in the fresh water of fast-flowing, gravelly-bed streams. After a few years feeding on worms, flies and other prey, they swim out to sea and become powerful predators there. Then they migrate back into fresh water, to the streams where they grew up, to produce their own eggs. It can take more than five years before a salmon returns to its home stream, finding its way by detecting the scent of the natural substances in its waters.

Bendy eel
The eel's body is long and flexible, allowing it to creep under rocks or nose about in mud in order to find food.

Male salmon provides sperm

Slim, smooth and sleek

The water of lakes and rivers is much 'thicker' than air, and more difficult and tiring to move through. Creatures such as salmon, eels and other fish, and mammals like otters and mink, can move fast through water because they have a slim and streamlined shape. Fish wave their tails from side to side to propel themselves forwards. Otters kick with their feet, and the flaps of skin called webs between the toes make a larger area to push back against the water, and so thrust the otter forwards.

Twist and turn

River otters swim at great speed, twisting around in a split second as they chase prey. The main forward force comes from pushing with its rear webbed feet. The front feet are held against the body except when moving slowly, when the otter paddles with all four feet.

Thick outer fur has waterproofing oils

Strong leg muscles kick rear webbed feet

Eel has long dorsal fin on top of body and anal fin along bottom

All tail

The eel seems to be almost all tail. It wriggles its body from side to side in waves that pass from front to back, to swim forwards. It can do the same but with waves passing from rear to front, to swim backwards. It also undulates along the lake bed like a snake.

Feeling the way

The otter's bushy whiskers can feel the way in muddy water, to detect prey such as worms and shellfish by touch. When swimming fast, the otter stretches its head and neck out forwards to make its front end more pointed and streamlined.

Otter floats on its back as it rests or eats its meal

Fast water

Rainbow trout are fish of fast-flowing streams, where the water contains plenty of dissolved oxygen. Some kinds stay in fresh water all their lives. Steelhead rainbows migrate out to sea, like salmon, and then return to breed.

Dense underfur keeps otter warm

No need for speed

Hippos are large, powerful animals with few enemies. They eat plants, so have little need to move fast. A hippo is not at all streamlined, being wide with a huge, blunt head.

Muscular tail swishes from side to side to help otter swim

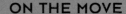

Large red damselfly, like all damselflies, holds its wings together over its back when resting

Flying in formation
Geese often travel on long flights in a V-shaped formation. Each goose saves energy by obtaining some lifting force due to the air pushed back by the goose in front. The flock changes leader regularly to share the total effort.

A common goose
The greylag goose is the most common and widespread goose species across Europe and Asia. In some parts these geese are resident, staying all year. In other regions they are migratory, flying north for summer and south for winter.

Like all dragonflies, the emperor dragonfly holds its wings at its sides when at rest

Coot's large feet help it to swim and walk across water plants

Yearly journeys

Swamps, marshes, bogs and other wetlands teem with life during the summer, when plenty of sunlight encourages plant growth in the warm water. However, during the winter the water freezes and survival becomes much more hazardous. Some larger animals, especially birds, breed in the wetlands during summer but then journey or migrate away to more suitable places, to avoid the harsh cold season. They return next spring to breed again.

Swallows on the wing
Many kinds of swallows spend the winter far to the south, in Southern Africa. They fly more than 5000 km northwards to Europe in spring, often to the same nest site that they used the year before. Swallows feed and even sleep on the wing. They swoop up high to catch flying insects.

Dragonfly cannot migrate long distances so lifecycle is adapted to seasons

Long-distance journey

Swallows, geese and other long-distance bird travellers use various methods to find their way. Many navigate by the Sun, Moon, stars, landmarks, coastlines and prevailing winds. Some have a built-in compass, probably inside the brain, to sense the direction of the Earth's natural magnetic field.

Mating flight
Swallows swoop and twitter as part of their courtship, and even mate in mid-air.

Beak opens and closes in 'bill-snapping' action

Well-developed head crest in breeding season

Head looks up in 'sky-point' posture

Neck bent in 'bow' posture

Dance of the herons
Herons carry out a ritual 'dance' for their partners. This helps each bird to check that the other is fit and healthy, and a suitable mate for breeding.

Courtship colours

The heron's beak and legs become brighter in colour during the breeding season when it is time to mate. It also moults its old feathers and grows new, brighter-coloured ones as part of its breeding appearance.

Air display
The marsh harrier flies very high, then dives at speed and somersaults in mid-air, to impress its mate in courtship flight.

Heron has long, spear-like beak to jab at food

Male harrier gives 'present' of food to female

Don't notice me

The male bittern's mating call is an extremely loud BOOM – almost like a cannon going off! However at other times the bittern is a very secretive bird, well camouflaged by its stripes and skygazing posture, amoung wetland reeds and rushes.

Sights and sounds for partners

As the breeding season arrives, most animals form pairs, ready to mate. Two important ways of attracting a partner are with sights and sounds. Birds carry out a complex series of displays as they stand and adopt postures, and also jump, 'dance' and fly in special ways. These displays are designed to show off their colourful feathers and are accompanied by songs and calls which add to the courtship effect.

Dragonfly eggs

Like frogs, dragonflies spend the first part of their life in water. A female dragonfly dips the rear end of her body under the surface to lay her eggs on the stems of water plants.

Altering shape

Marshes and swamps, with their mixture of water and land, are ideal places for frogs, toads and other amphibians. When young frogs hatch, they do not resemble their parents. They spend the first few weeks as long-tailed, legless tadpoles that live in water. They gradually change shape, grow legs, lose their tails and move on to land as adults.

Webbed feet

The adult frog has large rear feet with flaps of skin, or webs, between the toes. It swims by kicking its webbed feet, which form a large surface area to push hard against the water.

Front toes lack webs

Older tadpoles – one month

Dragonfly nymphs

The dragonfly's eggs hatch into young forms called nymphs. Like the tadpole, the nymph does not look much like its parent, lacking wings. But, like its parent, it is a fierce hunter of small prey.

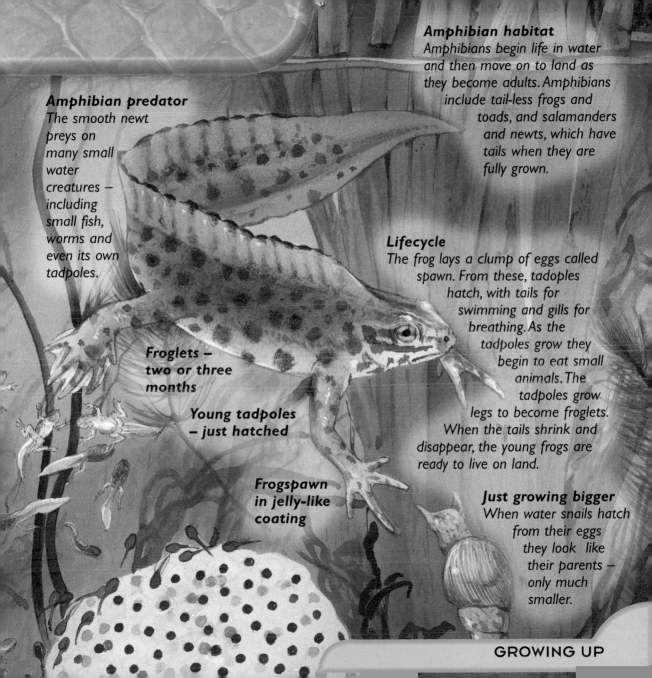

Amphibian habitat
Amphibians begin life in water and then move on to land as they become adults. Amphibians include tail-less frogs and toads, and salamanders and newts, which have tails when they are fully grown.

Amphibian predator
The smooth newt preys on many small water creatures — including small fish, worms and even its own tadpoles.

Lifecycle
The frog lays a clump of eggs called spawn. From these, tadoples hatch, with tails for swimming and gills for breathing. As the tadpoles grow they begin to eat small animals. The tadpoles grow legs to become froglets. When the tails shrink and disappear, the young frogs are ready to live on land.

Froglets — two or three months

Young tadpoles – just hatched

Frogspawn in jelly-like coating

Just growing bigger
When water snails hatch from their eggs they look like their parents — only much smaller.

Useful fish
The mosquito fish preys on the water-dwelling larvae of mosquitoes that would otherwise change into adults and become pests.

Leech asleep
In dry conditions the leech makes a case of slime or mucus around itself in the mud, and waits for its pond to fill again.

Very bendy, flexible body

More pointed front end has sucker and rasping, sharp-edged mouth

A sucker for blood
Swamps are home to various parasites – animals that live off others. Among such parasites are leeches. There are different types for each type of host animal, such as the fish leech, the pond-snail leech, and the medicinal leech which feeds on large mammals. To feed, the leech rasps a hole in the host's skin using its rounded mouth, edged with sharp, tooth-like spines. It sucks up the flowing blood and can swallow up to five times its own weight at one meal.

Rear sucker at wider, back end of body

A hungry hunter
A pond turtle moves slowly, but it preys on frogs, fish, water worms and snails. The turtle hides in weeds or buried in mud, and snaps at passing victims.

Shell gives protection and camouflage

Sharp, horny edging to jaws, for slicing up prey

Head, legs and tail can be drawn into shell

Surviving the drought

During a long, hot summer, some wetlands may start to dry out. The pools shrink and water creatures are crowded into smaller areas. The heat also drives oxygen from the water, so aquatic animals that breathe underwater by gills begin to suffocate. Some can cope with the drought by 'sleeping'. They enter a period of inactivity called aestivation, similar to hibernation. They burrow into the mud for protection and stay there until the autumn rains fill the pools again.

Two types of sleep
The European pond turtle spends the cold winter in hibernation, inactive in the mud at the bottom of the swamp. It wakes up in spring to feed and breed. But if the pools dry out, it enters aestivation and once again stays inactive on the bottom.

Mother and baby
Each baby gorilla sleeps with its mother in the tree nest she makes. Young gorillas stay with their mothers longer than almost any other animal, for three years or more, until the mother has her next baby. The mother gorilla grooms her offspring, removing dirt and pests from its fur and skin.

Evening tasks
As the gorilla troop settles for another night in the rainforest, most of the members climb into large trees, for safety from poisonous snakes and spiders, and from predators such as leopards. Each gorilla pulls and bends branches over to make a nest platform, where it can rest and sleep. The largest members of the group, the fully-grown adult males or silverbacks, may be too heavy to sleep in trees. So they stay on the ground, at the bases of the trunks, helping to protect the troop above.

Well groomed
Adult members of the group groom each other's fur. This strengthens bonds between the gorillas in the troop.

Gorillas are active in the early morning, rest and socialize during the day, and feed in the evening

Sealed in a nest

The female red-billed hornbill rears her chicks in a nest inside a rainforest tree-hole. The male blocks up the entrance with mud and twigs, leaving only a tiny slit, through which the female cannot leave her prison-like home — and predators cannot enter. The male bird passes food through the slit to his partner.

Waking up

As the gorillas, go to sleep, their tiny cousins, the bushbabies, are waking up. These nocturnal tree-dwellers leap through the branches with amazing speed and skill even on the darkest of nights.

Sleeping babies

Lesser bushbabies eat sap, bark, fruits, berries and small animals such as grubs. They sleep by day in a nest in a favourite forked branch, well hidden among the leaves.

Cooling down

Hummingbirds save energy as they sleep, by allowing their bodies to cool down by a few degrees. This is a kind of temporary night-time hibernation, called torpor. They warm up again at dawn, ready for action.

Beak and tongue

Each type of hummingbird has a particular shape of long, thin beak, designed to poke into certain kinds of flowers. The bird uses its long tongue to lick up and swallow the thick, sticky nectar.

Swapping places

By day in the rainforest, the air is busy with tiny, brightly coloured birds that dart about and hover in front of flowers. They are hummingbirds, and they probe with their long beaks into blooms, to sip up the sugary fluid called nectar. As dusk falls, the hummingbirds find a sheltered place to roost for the night. Their place is taken by bats, which are nocturnal (night-active) but do exactly the same as birds – hover in front of flowers to feed. Nectar-eating bats beat their wings fast to hover in front of flowers, as they lick up the sweet liquid.

Torpid hummingbird is still and silent, but cannot race away from predators

By night

Most bats are nocturnal and sleep by day in sheltered places such as tree-holes or caves. A few sleep out in the open, on tree branches or cliff faces. They rely on camouflage and keeping still for safety.

High energy

Fast flying and hovering uses up huge amounts of energy. Nectar, which is rich in sugars, is one of the few foods that can supply enough energy so that bats and hummingbirds can follow this lifestyle.

Bats roosting

The bats' hook-like leg claws grip their chosen roost perch. Bats usually roost in groups for warmth and safety. Each bat wraps its wings around its body for extra protection.

Busy woodpeckers

Golden-tailed woodpeckers usually live in female-male pairs. They make loud, harsh, laughter-like calls to each other, and at breeding time they chase each other up and down tree trunks.

Snake mates

Snakes cannot see or hear well, so usually the female releases a scent trail when she is ready to breed. The male detects this and follows. As he approaches her, he rubs his chin on her back and strokes her body to stimulate her, ready for mating.

Scents and strokes

The rainforest is a crowded habitat where bushes, trees, leaves and creepers obscure the view. So at breeding time here, many creatures use smells instead of sight displays to help them attract partners from far away. The smells waft through the jungle on the breeze and some creatures, such as certain male moths, can detect the scent from a female of their kind from over a kilometre away. When the pair come closer together, sight and then finally physical contact (or touch) take over as they court and prepare to mate.

Pair writhe together for touch stimulation

Pond in a tree

Some tree frogs never go down to the ground, even to lay their eggs. Instead, they use tiny pools of water in large flowers and forked branches, high in trees. The frog whips up the water into a foam to help camouflage the tadpoles.

African rock python lurks, camouflaged against rocks and tree trunks

Smelling tongue

A snake tastes and smell with its tongue. It flicks out the tongue to gather airborne scents and senses these in a special chamber in the roof of its mouth.

Scents in the night

Many male moths have very large, feathery antennae (feelers). These do not sense general smells and odours. Rather, they are specialized to detect only one main scent — the substance called a pheromone, given off by the female at breeding time.

Baby on the back

Some active rainforest animals, such as monkeys and bushbabies, carry their young around with them. The mother bushbaby leaves her tiny, newborn offspring in a tree nest for the first few days. Then she carries it gently in her mouth to a place where she can feed, and 'parks' the baby nearby on a twig. After a few weeks the youngster grows strong enough to cling to her fur. Gradually the young bushbaby learns to grasp twigs and climb by itself. It follows its mother at first, learning how she finds food and avoids falling.

Mother bushbaby pauses while feeding every now and then, to allow her baby to feed on her milk

Parked for the night

Bushbabies are named from their night-time calls, which sound like a human baby crying. When the mother 'parks' her youngster, it stays still and quiet so that it is not noticed by predators. She feeds nearby, then collects the baby, moves to a new feeding place, and so on through the night.

Large, long, strong back legs for leaping

Bushy tail wraps around body when sleeping

In the pouch

Some animals carry around their new babies in a special body part, the pocket-like marsupium or pouch. These animals are called marsupials and include kangaroos, wallabies, koalas, wombats and opossums. Marsupial babies are born tiny and almost helpless, eyes closed and without fur. All they can do is crawl to the pouch, attach to the mother's teat there, and suckle milk. They stay in the pouch for many weeks, developing and growing stronger. Eventually they are able to leave the pouch for short periods, to learn how to feed and move about on their own. But if a threat appears, they quickly return to the safety of the pouch.

Clinging tail
Some marsupials, such as the possum (below), have grasping or prehensile tails. They can hang by the tail while feeding or watching for danger.

Balancing tail
The bushbaby leaps with its body held upright, using its long tail for balance, and clinging on with its long-fingered hands.

First journey
A new-born kangaroo is only two centimetres long, but has to pull itself from the birth canal, up its mother's body to her pouch, to find a teat to attach to and suck.

The dusk change-over

As daylight fades in the woodland, there is a great change in animal activity. Diurnal (daytime) creatures such as warblers, hawks and butterflies settle down in a sheltered place among the leaves or roots, to roost or sleep. They are replaced by nocturnal animals such as owls, mice, bats and moths, which come out to look for food in the darkness. When light returns at dawn, the day and night shifts will change back again.

Birdsong
Warblers sing loudly at dusk and dawn. The sounds inform others that their territory is occupied.

Wings held back while singing

Back to the chicks
Parent warblers return to sit on their nests, built on or near the ground, and protect their young.

A long day
Golden-winged warblers spend most of the day searching twigs, leaves and bark for caterpillars, beetles, spiders and other small items of food. As dusk approaches they find a place to hide and rest.

Thin beak probes for insects

Sounds emerge through nose

Echoes detected by large ears

Low energy

As bats sleep by day, their internal body temperatures may fall by 5–10°C for a few hours, to save energy. This is an everyday version of the much longer, deeper sleep they undergo in winter, called hibernation. At dusk, the body temperature rises and the bat wakes up, ready to feed on moths, gnats and other nocturnal flying insects.

Bat wings

A bat's wings are really its hands. They are made of very thin, stretchy, leathery skin held out by the long bones of the fingers. The wings stretch down the side of the body to the legs. Bats usually only use their legs for hanging.

Sounding out the surroundings

Sounds are useful in woods, where lines of sight are often obscured by leaves and branches. Bats make high-pitched squeaks and clicks as they fly, which bounce off nearby objects. The returning echoes allow the bat to detect the position of objects around it in great detail, even when it is in total darkness. This is called echolocation. Whales, dolphins and fish also use echolocation to help them navigate.

Bat roosts

Bats sleep in old woodpecker nests, or similar holes inside trees, or in crevices between rocks, and even in underground caves.

Feeding new offspring

Many woodland creatures raise their young in safe, secure places like nests up in trees or burrows in the ground. The babies are too small to find their own food, so the parents feed them. Birds bring small, juicy items of food for their chicks. Their gaping mouths encourage the parents to feed them. Baby mammals such as badger cubs and deer fawns feed on milk from their mother.

Growing inside eggs

A baby bird inside its eggshell feeds on a yellow store of food called yolk. When it is time to hatch, the bird pecks through the shell.

Parents bring small caterpillars, grubs and other soft, juicy food

Chicks in the nest

Eastern bluebirds usually build their nest in an old woodpecker tree-hole or in the fork of a branch. The nest is shaped like a deep cup and made of grass and plant stems. The female incubates the eggs and the male brings food for her. Bluebird chicks are brown, and blend in well with the leaves and twigs so that the chicks are well camouflaged, and less likely to be noticed by predators.

Out of the burrow

When young badgers are about two or three months old they begin to come out of the burrow for short periods. They start to find their own food, and also roll and tumble together. This looks like playing. But the badgers are learning how to jump, pounce, run and carry out other actions important for their adult life.

In the burrow

Baby badgers spend the first two months safe in their deep burrow. Their underground home is called a sett. The mother leaves them in the sett while she goes to look for food.

Processed food

Like mammals, baby pigeons feed on mother's 'milk'. The pigeon can make a pale, cheesy substance in its crop (lower throat) which it regurgitates (brings up) as 'milk' for its nestlings.

Stag (male) and doe (female) deer begin to court

Claws are sharpened on tree trunk

Hidden fawn

The fawn stays perfectly still, hidden in the undergrowth, while its mother goes off to feed. The fawn's spots give camouflage among the leaves and stems. The mother deer returns to feed her fawn milk at regular intervals. Predators like wolves are more likely to spot the two together, rather than the fawn on its own, so she doesn't stay long.

Fawn begins to move and feed after four to six weeks

Badger food

The mother badger goes off hunting at night. She catches many kinds of small animals such as mice, voles, lizards and birds.

GROWING UP

Risky mating

Some male animals, including various spiders, run a great risk at breeding time — of being eaten by their partners. The female praying mantis is much larger than the male, and she may seize him even as he is trying to mate with her.

Egg parcel

Female spiders such as the black widow spin a strong case of silk thread, called a cocoon, to protect their eggs. The babies or spiderlings develop and hatch here but receive no further help from the parent.

Newly-hatched spiderling

Recycling silk

Most spiders spin a new web each day or night since the old one is soon damaged by prey, big animals or heavy rain. The spider eats its old web to recycle its materials.

Poison fangs

Sticky silk threads trap victim

Cocoon fixed securely to twig

Web among the leaves

Woodlands are ideal places for spiders, who spin their webs among the twigs and then wait nearby. When a fly, moth or similar victim gets trapped in the web, its movements alert the spider, who returns to bite the prey with its poisonous fangs.

Out on their own

Most young mammals and birds are cared for by their parents, but eventually they must leave their family and start life on their own. Insects, spiders and other similar creatures usually have no parental care after they hatch from their eggs. They must fend for themselves straight away. In the woodland, there are plenty of cracks and crevices among leaves, bark and roots where these small animals can hide. However danger lurks behind every leaf and twig, and most offspring are soon eaten.

Diadem spider builds large web in various shapes

Learning fast
Young mammals such as raccoons face many hazards. They may fall from a tree, or eat something which is harmful or poisonous. However, some foods, such as birds' eggs, are very nutritious and worth the risk of a daring climb. The youngster must learn quickly from its experiences to succeed in later life.

Deadly bite
The female black widow is one of the world's most dangerous spiders. She uses her venomous fangs to subdue prey, but she also bites larger animals or people in self-defence. Her poison is 15 times stronger than a rattlesnake's.

Notice me

Many hunted animals have fur that camouflages them in their surroundings. However, the skunk has a striking, easily-recognized pattern of bold black and white **fur**. The warning colours tell other animals that the skunk can spray a horrible-smelling fluid from its rear end to drive away potential attackers.

Long and flexible

The centipede's body is flattened, long and flexible so that it can wriggle under bark, leaves and stones. It is one of the speediest of the tiny animals on the forest floor.

A fast hunter

The weasel is one of the smaller hunting mammals. But it is fast and ferocious and tackles prey such as rabbits which may be larger than itself. Its usual victims are mice, voles and young birds. The weasel's body is lithe, long and flexible, so that it can follow mice down into their burrows to catch them. Short legs allow the weasel to move and turn quickly inside burrows.

Sharp senses

Mice, voles and other small hunted mammals have very large ears and eyes, so they can hear and see well to detect danger. They also have very speedy reactions to leap away from predators and scurry away through the leaves. A mouse detects nearby movements as vibrations in the ground.

Down from the branches

Squirrels leap with great skill through the tree-tops. They come down to the woodland floor, especially in autumn, to feed on fallen nuts and berries. At all times they are at risk from predators such as martens, which are also swift and agile.

Marten chases squirrel along a branch

Bushy tail helps squirrel to balance as it climbs

Centipede detects prey mainly by scent and touch, using its long antennae

Poison bite

The centipede hunts worms, snails, grubs and other woodland floor creatures. It has large poison fangs that can give a deadly bite, and sensitive feelers (antennae).

A miniature jungle

The woodland floor is a tangle of fallen sticks and twigs, roots, bits of bark and old leaves, loose soil and pieces of flowers and fruits. For the very small creatures like woodlice who live there, survival is just as difficult as for larger animals that walk or fly above. Predators such as centipedes may be little but they are fierce. They hide in the leaf litter, wriggling and slipping through the undergrowth to seek out their prey.

When death helps life

On the wide open grasslands, old or sick animals, or the leftovers from a lion or leopard kill, are soon spotted by hungry scavengers. Vultures, hyenas and jackals gather from far around, drawn by the sight and smell of the carcass. As they chew the skin, crunch the gristle, gnaw the bones and finish off the remains, they carry out the vital task of naturally recycling the dead body. Even the bones and teeth are picked over by ants, beetles and other tiny scavengers.

Chain reaction

Vultures circle in groups, evenly spaced apart. When one sees a likely meal it glides down. The others notice and follow, quickly drawing vultures from dozens of kilometres away.

Junior members of hyena clan wait their turn

The strongest bite

The spotted hyena has extremely strong jaws and powerful jaw muscles, and massive sharp-ridged cheek teeth. These work like shears to slice through skin, flesh and gristle. Hyenas can smell blood and meat from more than 10 km away.

Finding food

Lions usually make their own kills of fresh meat. But like other carnivores, they do not ignore an easier meal. A lion may chase a hyena, cheetah or leopard from its kill, and take over the carcass.

Ant bird perches on termite mound – a lookout place on the flat landscape

Keen eyes spot faraway victims

High view
The giraffe can see danger approaching, due to its very long neck and legs.

Long, probing neck
The vulture gets right inside the carcass with its long, flexible neck to peck up pieces of flesh with its sharp beak. The neck is mainly bare skin and lacks large feathers which would become soaked with blood.

FEEDING

Giant strides

Animals with long legs are able to run faster than short-legged ones, which is why so many grassland-dwellers have lengthy, slim limbs. In the giraffe's case, its extra-long legs help it to reach high into trees for leafy food.

Giraffes can reach more than 6 m high

Giraffes splay long legs to reach down and drink

Gazelles use tail flicks to warn each other of danger

Rapid runners

With few trees, bushes or rocks to get in the way, grasslands are home to some of the world's fastest land animals. The champion sprinter is the cheetah, accelerating to 100 km/h in under three seconds. However, top speed is not everything. Gazelles dart and zig-zag to dodge hunters like the cheetah. If the gazelle can stay ahead for more than about a minute, the cheetah gives up. It runs out of breath and risks overheating after its massive muscle-powered effort. A cheetah will not attempt a chase if its prey is too far away.

Need for speed

Even the largest animals are capable of sudden bursts of speed. A rhino can charge faster than a human can sprint, at more than 40 km/h. It uses its great bulk and sharp nose-horn to fight off almost any predator.

Sharp horns and hooves used for self defence

Safety in numbers

Herbivores such as Thomson's gazelles, giraffes and zebras live in herds for safety. As they feed or rest, one or two are always looking up, listening or scenting the air for danger. A warning snort or stamp alerts the whole herd.

Struggle for survival

The hunt is part of the natural survival of the fittest. Gazelles which are old, sick or injured are more likely to be caught. This keeps up the health and fitness of the main herd.

Ahead by a tail
The cheetah uses its tail as a rudder to turn at speed. Other grass- land animals use their tails to whisk away flies and to signal their moods and intentions.

Ant-birds feed on both ants and termites

Tunnels and ventilation holes allow cooling air to circulate around the nest

Big claws, long tongue

The aardvark rips open termite mounds and ant nests with the huge claws on its strong feet. It also uses these claws to dig its own home burrow, where it usually sleeps by day. It finds nests mainly by smell at night, but comes back to raid them in daylight when food is scarce. The aardvark licks up the tiny occupants inside the mound with its sticky tongue.

Feeling and scratching

Meerkats are day-active animals and their main sense is sight. However they also have well-developed whiskers, like night animals such as the aardvark. The whiskers help the meerkats to feel their way around their dark underground burrows. They also have strong claws to dig their burrows. Meerkats sit or stand upright on their mounds to get a better view of approaching danger.

Sealed in a nest

In addition to termites and ants, bees and wasps also make homes for themselves and their young grubs (larvae). The grubs are sealed inside six-sided containers or cells. They are fed by the adults on mashed-up worms, insects and similar food.

Aardvark's burrow

Burrow system has many escape exits

Dug-out soil piled into lookout mound

Fennec fox eats mainly termites which need little chewing, and so has small, weak teeth

Tunnels underground

Compared to a woodland with its tree-holes and roots, or a seashore with its weeds and boulders, there are few places to shelter on the grassland. Yet tiny, pale, soft-skinned insects called termites, that dry out and die quickly in the hot sun, survive here. They live inside huge mounds which they build by chewing and shaping the soft earth into towering walls which bake hard in the heat. Many other grassland creatures, from meerkats and aardvarks to mice, dig burrows and tunnels as homes in the soil.

A valuable patch of grassland

In some kinds of zebras, the stallion (male) must keep a patch of grassland, called his territory, and chase rival stallions from it. Mares (females) only stay and breed with a stallion who owns a territory. Here they can graze more peacefully, since the stallion also helps to defend them and their foals (young) from predators.

Meerkat's warning yip means possible threat nearby

Ready to fight
Stallions communicate their readiness to fight by snorting, tossing their heads and stamping their hooves.

Sandy-coloured fur gives camouflage against dry soil and brown grass stems

Kicking out
Rival stallions rear up and lash out at each other with their front hooves, or turn and kick with their back hooves. The winner takes over the territory and the harem (group) of females.

Puzzling stripes
Why the zebra has distinctive black and white stripes is not clear. At dusk and dawn, when most big predators are on the hunt, the stripes may help to camouflage the zebra in the tall grass.

Waiting for a result
The zebra mares wait for the conflict to end. A successful stallion may gather five or more females and keep his territory for more than five years.

Sharp teeth
Battling stallions may bite each other's necks as they fight for dominance of the harem.

Protective father

Unlike most birds, it is the male ostrich who makes the nest and cares for the eggs. He does not need to keep them warm by incubating (sitting on) them, since the hot desert sun does the job. But if a hungry egg-stealer comes near he stands over the eggs, waves his wings and hisses loudly, ready to attack.

Large white-tipped wing feathers make ostrich look big and fierce

Partners aplenty

The male ostrich, unlike most birds, has not one but several female partners. The most senior female and lays her eggs first, so they have the best chance of survival.

Females lack large wing feathers of male

Huge toe claws slash at enemies

Shared nest

The male ostrich scrapes a hollow in the ground and up to five females lay their eggs here. The nest may contain 15 or more eggs.

Need for speed

The ostrich cannot fly, but it is the fastest runner among the birds. Its long legs stride along at 70 km/h and so it easily escapes from most predators.

Nest defence

In harsh habitats such as deserts, food is scarce, and so creatures have to eat what they can, when they can. If a meat-eater like a jackal comes across a likely meal, perhaps an ostrich egg, it tries to take advantage. But the ostrich is just as ready to put up a fierce defence. It flaps, pecks and kicks, to communicate to the jackal: 'Leave my offspring alone'.

While the parent's away
Most parent birds cannot stay with their eggs all the time, since they must go off to feed. And reptile eggs are simply left by the female. Desert lizards such as the gila monster move in as soon as a nest is unguarded.

Stone's throw
An ostrich egg has a very thick shell which most birds cannot crack with their beaks. But the Egyptian vulture uses a tool. It drops a stone on to the egg to break it.

Crouching low
The jackal's cowering posture communicates that it will probably not attack the nest.

The vulture can lick out the soft contents of the broken egg

Prickly meals

Food is so scarce in the desert, that almost any plant is at great risk of being eaten. This is why so many desert plants, such as cacti and acacia, have thorns, spines and prickles to repel herbivores. But herbivores are equipped with tough mouths, hard lips and strong teeth to tackle their spiky food. Since trees are rare in the desert, many small animals dig burrows to find shade in the heat of the day.

Smaller herbivores
Prickles and spines do little to deter small plant-eaters such as the rainbow grasshopper. It can crawl among the sharper parts of plants to munch the softer bits between them.

Egret pecks pests off oryx's skin

Egret warns oryx of approaching danger

Male's horns may be more than 100 cm long

Fencing for females
In the breeding season, male oryx clash their long horns as though fencing with swords. They are battling for dominance so that they can mate with females in the group.

Egrets feed on insects disturbed by oryx

Versatile horns
The oryx uses its horns not only for battling rivals and in self-defence, but also to scratch in the desert soil. This exposes roots to eat, or makes a hollow where water may collect.

Finding food
Oryx rarely stay in one place. Plants are so few and far between in the desert that these antelopes are continually on the move, wandering dozens of kilometres by night when it is cooler, to find fresh grazing.

Acacia thorns repel browsing animals

Balancing tail
The kangaroo rat's long tail helps it to balance as it leaps across the desert sand.

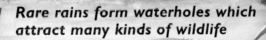

Rare rains form waterholes which attract many kinds of wildlife

Storing seeds
Kangaroo rats and similar small rodents collect seeds to store in their burrows.

FEEDING

Shifting sands

Desert sands and soils are loose and shifting, and slip as animals try to run over them. So desert creatures have different ways of moving. The desert sidewinding viper throws its body into a series of sideways loops. The sand skink wriggles like a fish and swims through the sand grains. The desert whiptail lizard has very long toes fringed by wide scales. These work like sandshoes to spread its weight so that it does not sink into the soft surface.

Looking for prey

The sidewinding viper half-buries itself in the sand at a suitable place, to wait for passing victims such as gerbils, kangaroo rats or small lizards. In this position it is partly hidden from both prey and the heat of the sun. Like other vipers it has a poisonous bite.

Tough scales protect skink from sharp, rubbing sand particles

Swimming in sand

The sand skink can walk like a normal lizard using its four strong legs. But in very loose sand it folds its legs and feet against the sides of its body, and arches itself from side to side. It wriggles through the sand like a worm in mud.

Hard, pointed nose pushes through soil

Tracks in the sand

The sidewinding viper pushes its long body sideways against the sand, which makes it less likely to slide about on the grains. It leaves a series of J-shaped ridged marks that look like tyre tracks.

No need for speed

The desert tortoise moves slowly and purposefully and so slips less on loose sand. Its scaly skin and domed shell give excellent protection against sun and predators.

Toes cool in air flow

Any spot of shade

Lizards, insects and similar animals take advantage of any patch of shade, near a rock or small plant, where they can rest and keep cool.

Hard scales protect against touch of hot rocks and sand

Opposing front and rear legs held up at same time

The burning sand

Creatures out in the scorching sun, can be burned by the hot surface of the sand. The desert whiptail lizard alternately lifts pairs of legs off the ground so its feet can cool in the air.

The driest nursery

The desert is a dangerous place to live – and an even more dangerous place to raise offspring. Starvation, drought, predators and overheating are just a few of the risks facing young animals. This is why so many desert creatures show parental care, including mammals and birds, but also creatures like scorpions. They protect their young in a safe place such as under a rock, in a burrow, or in the scorpion's case, on the mother's back, directly under her deadly tail sting.

Growing inside eggs

Many snakes lay their eggs and leave them to hatch alone. But the female python coils around her clutch of eggs and guards it until the babies emerge.

Fierce hunters

The desert sun-spider (solifuge) is not a true spider and lacks a poison bite. But its pincer-like fangs tackle small lizards, birds and desert rodents.

A venomous bite

All true spiders have eight legs and two large, poison-injecting fangs to subdue their prey. Many hide in holes during the day.

Pincer-like fangs

Cartwheels

To escape danger and reach safety the sun-spider curls up its legs and rolls like a ball down the sand dune.

Out at night
Desert scorpions, like scorpions from other habitats, are nocturnal – active mainly at night. They have very poor eyesight but are they extremely sensitive to touch, movements and vibrations. They detect vibrations in the ground using feather-like parts called pectines on the underside of the body.

Tail arches over body when scorpion is threatened

Poison glands in last tail segment

Simple eyes detect mainly light and dark

Two front limbs specialized as pincers

Small predators
As soon as the baby scorpions are born, they can sting and hunt tiny prey.

Powerful fangs

Piggy-back ride
Young scorpions do not hatch from eggs. They are born fully formed and ride on their mother's body for a time, safe just under her poisonous sting. They leave her back after one or two weeks.

Stung to death
A scorpion uses its sting mainly in self-defence but it may also jab prey to stop it struggling. It hunts insects such as grasshoppers, spiders, and small mammals and birds.

Owls out by day

Most owls hunt at night, under cover of darkness. But nights in the flat, treeless tundra lands of the far north are too long, dark and cold for animals to be out and about, and an owl would have nothing to catch at night. So the snowy owl hunts by day over the tundra. It glides silently and swoops down to grab victims in its talons (claws). It carries the prey to one of its favourite perches and tears it up to eat with its strong, hooked beak. At breeding time, it must catch more prey so that it can give some to its chicks in the nest.

White for winter

Many creatures in cold northern lands, like the ptarmigan and Arctic hare, have white fur or feathers. They blend in with ice and snow, so that they can be seen less easily. Merging with the surroundings is called camouflage.

Brown for summer

The ptarmigan's feathers change to brown in summer, for better camouflage among grass stems and earth. In spring the Arctic hare's white winter fur falls out and brown summer fur grows back to replace it. This change is called moulting.

Warm in the water

The polar bear may plunge into the icy water to catch seals. Its long fur coat and a thick layer of blubber (fat) under its skin keeps it warm.

Family meal

Snowy owls prey on lemmings, voles, baby hares, small birds and similar creatures. Their white plumage is camouflage against the snow-laden clouds, allowing them to dive down from above on to their victims more effectively.

Hunting in the dark

Most owls, like the great horned owl, are active at night. They detect prey by sight with their huge eyes and with their amazing hearing.

Not quite white
The male snowy owl is mainly white with a few stripes or bars. The female is more barred.

Tail feathers fan out on landing, acting as a brake

Nesting in the open
The owl chicks are protected in their nest in the open by their mother.

Heading north

The tundra has a short summer, when the snow melts and grasses, mosses and other plants grow. This sudden abundance of food brings a variety of animals who migrate long distances from the south. Birds such as geese and terns can travel quickly by flight. Larger animals such as caribou can walk over several weeks.

The longest journey

Arctic terns make the longest migrations of any animal. As the summer ends in the Arctic, they fly south more than 20,000 km to the Antarctic – where summer is just beginning.

Grazing geese

Canada geese feed by grazing – pecking at grasses and mosses, and the water plants in shallow, marshy pools.

Paired for breeding

The female and male geese stay together to raise their family. They may keep together as a pair for several years.

Tern hovers to spot food or danger

Risks of migration
Caribou (also called reindeer) trek hundreds of kilometres north to feed on the tundra plants. When the cold and snow return they will grow thicker fur and migrate south again, for winter in the shelter of the forests. Wolves follow their migration, to pick off the old, weak and sick.

Unlike other deer, both male and female caribou have antlers

Finding food

Plants grow sparsely on the tundra, and caribou and musk oxen soon eat most of the lush vegetation in one area. They can either move on to find fresh grazing, or scrape with their hooves to reveal mosses, roots and lichens.

Two fur coats
Musk oxen stay out on the open tundra during the winter. They are kept warm by their thick fur. The outer coat has tough, strong hairs almost 100 cm long. Beneath is the dense, softer fur of the undercoat.

Bushy tail wraps around fox when asleep, for extra warmth

Howls tell other wolf packs to keep away

Food from the freezer
The Arctic fox is one of the few animals that can live out on the tundra all year round, due to its thick fur. It often scavenges on the bodies of dead sea animals.

Tail held up, growl and ears pricked shows dominance

Crouching, lowered tail, whimper and flattened ears show submission

Leader of the pack

Wolves live in groups called packs. They hunt on their own for small prey, like lemmings and mice. The pack bands together to catch large animals such as caribou and musk oxen. Members of the pack also help each other to stay safe, produce young and keep on the move. One male and one female wolf are the dominant pair or leaders of the pack. They communicate with others by body postures using their faces, ears, legs and tails, and by sounds such as snarls and yelps, almost as if talking.

Almost a fight
Sometimes a younger wolf challenges one of the pack leaders with bared teeth and snarls. But it's mainly a show of strength. The wolves rarely fight. If they did, they could be wounded and soon die on the cold tundra. Many animals put on shows like this called ritual displays but rarely get into a real battle.

Summer coat is lighter and thinner than winter fur

Living alone

A wolf pack can hunt large prey together. The polar bear hunts alone. It creeps over the snow towards a seal, or waits by a hole in the ice for it to come up and breathe, then grabs the seal's head in its teeth.

On the scent

Wolves use their keen noses to smell prey. They can scent a dead, rotting carcass of a seal or whale from 5 km away. When one wolf begins to move, the others follow. Their long legs allow the wolves to 'dog-trot' for hours to tire out victims or track down food.

Standing tall

The chief or alpha wolf stands tall and growls at the less senior members of the pack, to keep them in their place. But as soon as its growls sound weak or faltering, a challenger may come forward.

COMMUNICATION

Active by day

Wolves and geese are diurnal, meaning they are active mainly during daylight, although hungry wolves may become nocturnal and hunt at night.

Wolf is bitten by mosquitoes and scratches its bites

Active by night

Lemmings are nocturnal, meaning they are active mainly at night. They come from their burrows at dusk, as it gets dark. They feel their way in the dark night, and inside their tunnels, using the long hairs on their noses, called whiskers. Small ears, blunt nose and rounded shape prevent heat loss.

Second thoughts

A wolf on its own may not risk trying to attack a goose or steal its eggs or chicks. The geese gather round to flap and peck at the intruder The wolf's lowered tail shows it may soon retreat.

Parasitic mites live in goose feathers

Canada goose stands its ground against threat of wolf

Busy eaters

Lemmings eat all kinds of plant food such as leaves, stems, and even hard seeds and roots. They gnaw with their long, sharp front incisor teeth, which, like those of many other rodents, keep growing so they never wear down.

Safe by day

Lemmings sleep by day in tunnels they dig in the soil. They also flee there if threatened by a predator such as an Arctic fox, snowy owl or wolf – or by gnats, mosquitoes or other parasites.

Parasite pests

Apart from mosquitoes, several other kinds of small creatures are blood-sucking parasites. They include gnats, which are flies like mosquitoes, and mites (right), tiny cousins of spiders, also with eight legs.

Tiny blood-suckers

Some animals who feed on other creatures are large and powerful, like wolves. Others are tiny, like the mosquito. This small fly is not a hunter but a parasite. It feeds by taking nourishment from another animal, the host, without killing it. Mosquitoes bite animals and suck their blood. Their hosts vary from lemmings and voles to huge caribou or even birds such as geese. The swampy bogs of the tundra are ideal breeding places for mosquitoes, whose larvae (grub-like young) live in water.

Sharp needle

A mosquito has a mouth shaped like a hollow needle, to pierce the host's skin and suck up its blood. It finds the thinnest area of skin to pierce.

FEEDING

Flying high

Flight is the fastest way for animals to move about, especially over the rocks, cliffs, crags and steep slopes of the mountains. Birds can rise to great heights to look for food along the mountain range. They can also fly quickly down to the more sheltered foothills during storms or in winter, to avoid the worst weather.

Primary feathers

Secondary feathers

Types of wing feathers

The large primary feathers at the end of a bird's wing are fanned and twisted for delicate control. The secondary feathers nearer the body are curved to produce an upwards force or lift (just like the wing of a plane).

Wings for soaring

As wind blows against mountain slopes it gets pushed upwards, creating rising columns of air. Birds such as eagles, condors and vultures glide round and round in these to gain height without even having to flap their wings.

Control in the air

The eagle uses its wings and tail to control its flight speed and direction. As the wind whistles past and buffets the bird around, the eagle continuously tilts its tail from side to side to keep its flight steady. The tail feathers fan out to slow the speed of the eagle's flight.

Contour feathers cover body

Useful feathers
Feathers not only form flying and control surfaces, but give a smooth outline to the bird's body, to improve streamlining. They also provide patterns and colours. The golden eagle is well camouflaged against the brown mountain rocks.

Smooth leading edge to wing

Highest nests
Some birds nest so high in the mountains, their chicks are safe from almost any predator. The alpine chough breeds at an altitude of more than 4000 m.

Killing claws
The eagle's long, strong toes are as big as your fingers and tipped with very hard, sharp claws called talons. These are for grabbing prey such as voles, rabbits, hares and even baby deer.

Feet and toes are protected by scales

ON THE MOVE

Butterfly of the mountains

The apollo butterfly is found in mountains across Europe and Asia. It basks on a rock in the morning sunshine to warm up after the chilly night, then flies to look for flowers, where it feeds on their sweet nectar. Its wings need to flap strongly to cope with the mountain winds.

Female

Male

Antennae

Front wing partly overlaps rear wing

Butterfly wings

Most insects, including butterflies, have four wings (except flies, which have two). The two overlapping wings on each side flap up and down as one. The wings are covered with tiny scales of different colours that make up the bright patterns.

Scents in the night

Butterflies, like many other animals, use smells as well as sights to attract a mate. The female produces an invisible scent called a pheromone that wafts through the air. The male detects the scent with his long, club-tipped *antennae* (feelers).

Bright hues send important messages

Colours and patterns are very important for many kinds of animals, to convey messages to others. This is especially important on mountains, where the air is clear and the views wide open. Many bright colours are designed to attract mates at breeding time. As the apollo butterfly flits across the slopes in the summer sunshine, its wing patterns flash on and off like glowing lights to attract a partner. Other colours are designed to do the opposite and warn others, especially predators, to stay away.

Courtship calls

Female crickets make use of their long **antennae** to hear mating calls at breeding time. The male cricket chirps loudly, by rubbing the veins on his front wings together, to gain the attention of the female.

How butterflies breed

After courtship and mating, a female butterfly such as the apollo lays her eggs on the type of plant which the caterpillars will eat when they hatch out. This is called their 'food plant'. The caterpillars (larvae) busily eat and grow, shedding their skins about five times. Then they change into inactive, hard-cased chrysalises (pupae). After a few weeks the chrysalis case splits open and the adult butterfly crawls out.

Warning colours

The caterpillars of butterflies and moths move slowly and cannot run away from danger. So many are brightly coloured as a warning to predators that they have horrible-tasting flesh or foul-flavoured body fluids. Predators soon

Apollo caterpillar feeds mainly on the mountain stonecrops – its 'food plant'

Asleep for the winter

Winters are particularly long and cold on mountains, where snow and ice cover the slopes. Many creatures hide away during this time, in crevices and caves among the rocks, or in burrows they dig for themselves. Warm-blooded mammals such as marmots enter a deep winter sleep called hibernation. Cold-blooded creatures like snakes are simply too chilled to move. As the spring warmth increases they wake up and are soon ready to feed and breed.

Communal den

Garter snakes spend the winter inactive, in a sheltered hole where the frost and ice cannot reach to freeze them solid. A hole is often used by several snakes, year after year. When the snakes stir from their torpor, they may mate in the den.

The male snakes writhe over the female at mating time

The female snake is larger than the males

Underground village

Marmots spend the winter huddled together in their sleeping chamber. Their body temperatures drop from about 40°C to only 6°C, to save energy.

Furry marmots
Mountain mammals like marmots have very thick fur to keep out the cold, strong winds. The fur grows even longer and thicker in winter for extra warmth.

Food for winter

Like many animals which endure cold winters, the mountain beaver prepares by gnawing twigs and bushes, and storing the pieces inside its burrow under a large tree. This store of plant material should provide enough food to last the beaver through the winter.

Spring clean
When marmots wake in spring, they groom their fur so that it stays in good condition to keep them warm. Each marmot combs its fur thoroughly with its claws and teeth.

Marmot stands on hind legs to look for danger

Fur covers most of body and legs to keep in heat

SLEEPING

Battling for mates

In herd animals such as bighorn sheep, the breeding season is a period of fierce battles. The males head-butt each other to show who is strongest and most healthy. The females mate with the winners, so that their offspring are more likely to be strong and healthy. The mountains echo with the crashes and clatters of the males, or rams, as they bash their foreheads and horns together. The females and young keep their distance from all the fighting and graze quietly.

Big horns
The bigger a male bighorn's horns, the more dominant or senior he is likely to be. Females have smaller horns. So do younger males, that are not yet mature and ready to breed.

Strong skull and neck bones absorb jolts

Male rears up on back legs and lunges forward to butt

Strong neck and shoulder muscles increase butting force

Fight to the death
Usually one male bighorn is more powerful that its rival, and the contest is soon over. However, if two males are more evenly matched, they may head-butt each other for hours. Sometimes they become so dazed that they are knocked out, and one may become so injured that it dies.

Old enough to fight
Young male bighorns do not mature until they are seven or eight years old. The young females are mature at four years old.

The rutting season
Various kinds of sheep, goats, deer and antelopes have battles between rival males at mating time. This is called the rutting period. In animals with branched antlers, such as bull elk (above), the antlers may become locked together and then both contestants die.

Strong legs and feet for leaping up crags and over boulders

Gripping hooves
Mountain hoofed animals such as bighorns have strong hooves with wide, roughened bases. These help to grip the rocks, especially when they are icy and slippery in winter.

Living alone
In some herd animals such as sheep and deer, the males live on the fringes of the group. In elephants, older males usually live alone and only meet the females briefly at mating time.

GLOSSARY

Aestivation Period of inactivity during the summer.

Amphibian An animal that lives partly on land and partly in the water.

Aquatic Living in water.

Camouflage Disguise produced by colour, pattern or shape, which makes an animal difficult to see.

Carnivore An animal that eats mainly or entirely meat.

Habitat The particular area or natural place where a group of plants or animals live. Examples are deserts, lakes and grassland.

Herbivore An animal that eats only plants.

Hibernation When animals go to sleep for the winter. The animal lives off its stored fat reserves until the spring.

Incubate To brood eggs, to hatch young.

Larva The grub of an insect.

Life cycle The stages through which a creature passes from fertilization to death.

Marsupial A mammal whose young complete their development inside their mother's pouch.

Migration The regular journey to a place in order to breed or find better food supplies.

Parasite A plant or animal that depends completely on another plant or animal in order to stay alive.

Plankton Tiny animals that live in salt or fresh water.

Predator An animal that gets its food by hunting and killing other creatures.

Reptile A cold-blooded scaly animal that lays eggs on land; a few give birth to live young. Reptiles include lizards, snakes and turtles.

Scavenger An animal that feeds on the flesh of dead animals (carrion).

Tundra The Arctic region of treeless land, the soil is frozen apart from the surface layer, which melts in the summer.

Vegetation The collective term for vegetable growth including plants, trees and flowers.

INDEX